BOE

World

BOB BERRY on PENDINE

World Land Speed Record

Lynn Hughes

Produced and printed in Wales
for Golden Grove
at the Gomer Press
Llandysul
Ceredigion

ISBN: 1 85902 702 4

Available at The Museum of Speed, Pendine, Carmarthenshire
Distributed through the Welsh Books Council, Glanyrafon Estate, Aberystwyth, Ceredigion SY23 3AQ

Forthcoming by the same author:
Pendine Races: the text
Pendine Races: in pictures
(Fifty Years of Motor Racing on Pendine Sands in two volumes)

Contents

Illustrations

Frontispiece: Bob Berry, motor cycle racing-driver (490cc Norton International) c1937

1: First Gear

Bob Berry was born in Skipton, North Yorkshire, around 1908. As a young man he admired the prowess of local racing motor cycle driver, JH 'Jack' Carr. Winner of the Manx Grand Prix, Carr was a celebrated amateur whose stylish performances on his 998cc Brough Superior, model SS100 'Pendine', thrilled the crowds at sand-race meetings throughout the North - at Southport, Redcar and Blackpool. This machine, in sand-racing trim, powered by an 8/50 JAP-engine, had been ACU certified at 110.74mph, in one direction, over the 'flying kilometre' on Southport, in September, 1932.

At Pendine, JH Carr successively won the Welsh Speed Championship 'Hundred Mile' with his fabulous Brough, in 1931and 1932.

Determined to emulate his hero, Berry, an experienced sand-racer, managed to acquire this

JH Carr in action at Pendine, August 1932

famous racing motor cycle from Broughs when Jack Carr retired from racing in 1936. It had the reputation of being the most successful racing Brough Superior ever to leave the Haydn Road, Nottingham, works - with over a hundred 'Firsts' to its name. Bob Berry, in business as a garage proprietor in Manchester, raced it locally and competed in Speed Championships on Pendine with it after the War (with, it must be said, no

Jack Carr, Pendine 1932

more conspicuous success than second place in a single one-mile sprint).

During the war, Bob Berry's Manchester garage and his tyre business had both succumbed to Luftwaffe bombs. Abandoning racing at the age of 39, he determined thereafter to 'avenge his ruination on the perfidious Hun' by reclaiming for Britain the World Land Speed Record for a motor cycle. The 1937 'Flying Kilometre' record continued (in 1949) to be held on German soil by a German machine at 173.67 mph.

Ernst Henne had averaged this impressive best of two opposite runs on the autobahn at Frankfurt-am-Main on the 'Kompressor', a 493cc, supercharged (90 - 95bhp), streamlined BMW. It was a tremendous speed for its time and a hard act to follow. Berry was against the idea of mechanically-forced induction and was intent on upholding the honour of British engineering on a normally-aspirated machine, albeit one of twice the BMW's engine capacity.

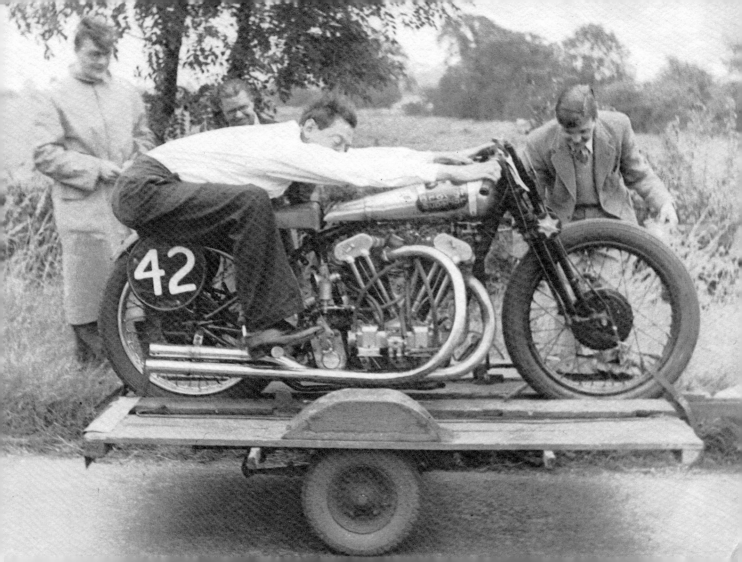

p.11 Having taken delivery of the JH Carr Brough (8/50 JAP engine), in 1936

p.12 Getting to know the Carr racing machine, 1936

The Motor Cycle, in 1949, was offering a trophy and an award of £500 to the first British rider of a British machine who could bring the record back to this country. To this purpose Bob Berry dedicated the rest of his active life.

This is why there was motor cycle speed activity on Pendine beach early one morning in April, 1949. The unmistakable double-echo of a highly-tuned JAP engine thrilled up the beach and then down again, as Bob Berry and his little team from Manchester tested a Brough Superior for a crack at the World Land Speed Record for motor cycles. The bicycle he was riding was JH Carr's 'Pendine', fitted with a replacement JAP model 8/75(bhp) engine.

Berry was intent on reclaiming for Britain the

record previously held by Englishman Eric Fernihough on a Brough at Gyon, Hungary, in April, 1937 (169.78 mph). Later that same year Ernst Henne broke Fernihough's record; then Fernihough was killed in a subsequent attempt to reclaim it. The 'Flying kilometre' record for motor cycles had been a preoccupation in Britain since the early days of motoring, progressively being raised from WE Cook's record of 75.92 mph on the 16th June, 1909 - on a 994cc NLG - by such heroes as CR Collier (Matchless), Jake de Rosier and Herbert le Vack (Indians) to CF Temple's 108.48 mph on a camshaft 996cc British Anzani, at Brooklands on 6th November, 1923. That was the last (World) 'Flying kilo' record for motor cycles to be held on British soil.

Berry made yet another engine change. The SM Greening-designed 8/80 engine for JA Prestwich of Tottenham (JAP) had a performance curve such that it was faster in second (of three gears) than a previous 8/75 had been in top (124mph). At Brighton Speed trials in 1947, the 8/80, in Berry's hands, reached 128 mph in second gear, crossing the finishing line at 140 mph in third - when it was still nowhere near 'flat-out'.

Engine-power was not the nub of the matter, though it was generally conceded that 100 bhp was the minimum requirement to push a machine weighing 400 - 500lbs beyond 180mph. *The Motor Cycle* identified the related problems:[1]

Chief among them are achieving the requisite brake horse-power, and ensuring directional stability at speeds on the exciting side of three-miles-a-minute - faster than man has ever travelled before on two wheels. Unstreamlined machines capable of providing something like 100 bhp even after extensive testing are rare, and enormous development work would be necessary before adequate power and reliability could be obtained from any one of them. To take an existing machine capable of providing enough power and attempt to modify it for full streamlining, which, one imagines, would demand a prone position, would give rise to a host of questions, the answers to which are largely unknown.

On the Jabbecke Motorway in Belgium, in 1949, Berry was to capture the national speed record of 155.9 mph on the Brough in bad weather conditions and twilight gloom, without the fairing. Stability, he felt, was a severe problem, but things were progressing.

[1]*The Motor Cycle*, 17 February, 1955.

p.15 Bob Berry racing the Brough at Pendine. Easter, 1946 (LA Lusardi photo)

p.16 Berry working on an 8/80-engined version, 1949

p.17 Admirers crowd around. Pendine, 1949

p.18 Posing with the Brough 8/80, 1949 (LA Lusardi photo)

p.19 At full-chat in second

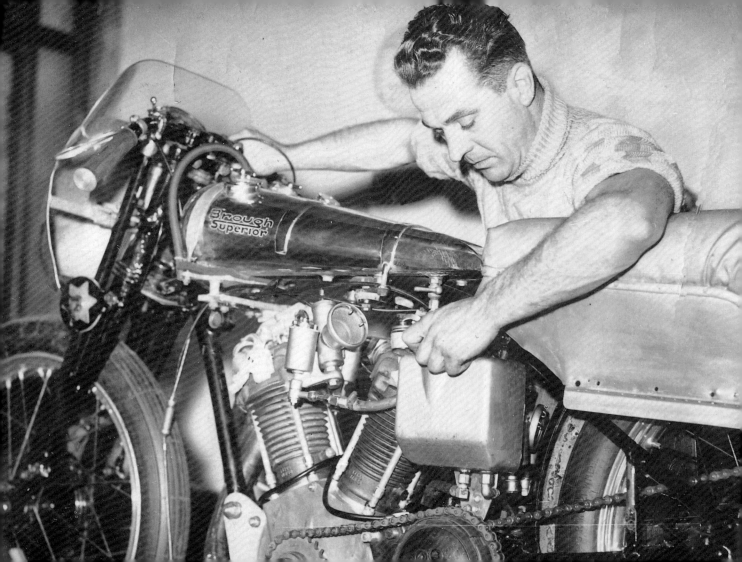

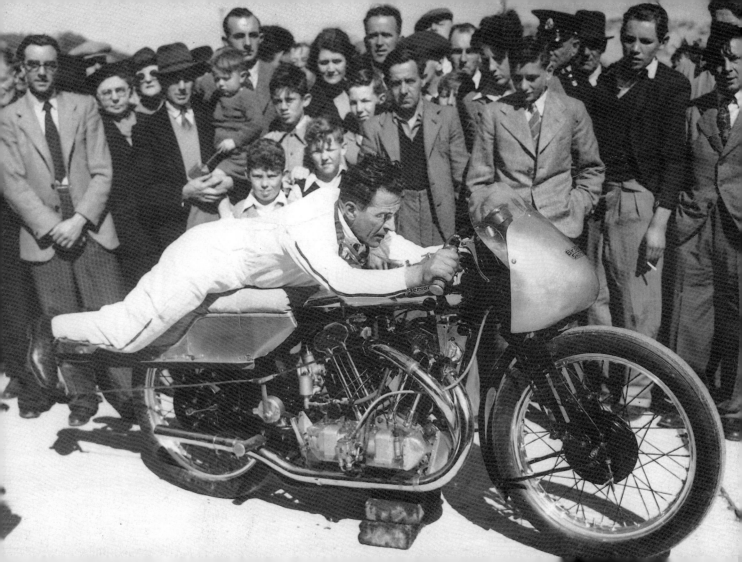

To Rosemary
With best wishes
Bob Berry.

2. Into Second

When he came down to Pendine from Chorlton-on-Medlock in the spring of 1949, Berry decided not to test his machine in streamlined guise. Instead, he had devised a fairing arrangement which enabled him to lie in a prone position, on a 3ft-long Dunlopillo pad, 'to minimise wind-resistance'. The JAP 8/80's engine-power was up to between 84 and 86 horse-power on the bench, at 6000rpm against the brake, after polishing and altering compression-ratios.

On each side of the rear wheel are duralmin T-section horizontal girders, at the rear of which is a cross-bar with footrests; there is also a pivoted gear-change pedal on the off-side. The gear-change technique is interesting. A hand-change lever is fitted near the front of the tank. It is coupled to a relay lever near the rear of the tank, the foot-change being connected to the same lever. From the relay lever a rod changes the motion to the positive-stop gear-change mechanism which controls the Sturmey-Archer three-speed box.

First gear is engaged by hand, the machine starts and accelerates, and the change from first to second is also made by hand. At something approaching 90 mph, the changed to top gear is made and this is done with the foot. If necessary, foot pressure can be maintained on the pedal to prevent jumping out. Downward changes, as the machine decelerates after its measured distance has been completed will be made by hand.

For the record attempt, special dural rims and shallow-ribbed racing tyres have been supplied by Dunlop, the size being 3.50 x 21 inch[2].

Bob Berry was an unashamed patriot, and very conscious of being the last in a long and great

The shell fitted, 1949

Bob Berry racing his 490 International Norton at Pendine.
(LA Lusardi photo)

Bob Berry

tradition of Brough Superior riders. He did not want to let them, George Brough or Britain down.

Despite all endeavours, the weather took a hand - as it so often did at Pendine when record bids were afoot - and the time-keepers booked for Saturday and Sunday, April 2nd and 3rd, did not even get to lick their pencils. In a way it was as well, because there were 'Number 2 cylinder lubrication problems'. With the very high compression ratios (13 to 1), the rear cylinder was tending to seize.

*

Bob Berry was back in the second week of August, 1949, for another crack at the *Motor Cycle* Land Speed Record prize.

A keen wind blew in off the sea, and Berry was content to cruise his machine back. He expressed himself pleased with the day's work

p.22 'The Kneeler'

... On Thursday evening, (he) made another unofficial run in each direction along the beach. In spite of a strong off-shore wind and unfavourable sand conditions, the test was very successful. The Manchester man said later that the rev counter of his machine had a speed well in excess of the record.

On the following evening, disaster nearly overtook Berry when he was flashing over the beach at approximately 120 mph in second gear. A patch of soft sand situated a little off the course he would be using for the record attempt caused his front wheel to wobble perilously. The performance of the machine, however, pleased him, and he decided to make an attack on the world's record of 174 mph early on Sunday morning.

Early on Saturday, Berry made several short runs over the beach for a magneto test. He said afterwards that he had reached 7 000 revs in bottom gear.

Keen disappointment was expressed on Sunday morning when a thick coastal mist blanketed the beach, and the attempt was held up until the evening between high and low water. However, the state of the beach was too rippled for an attack in the evening, and Berry decided to wait another few tides before making his speed dash.

But conditions did not permit another attempt. That ended Berry's ambition to bring the motor cycle 'Flying kilometre' record back onto British soil. Events were to take a turn.

[2]*The Motor Cycle*, 31st March, 1949.

3. Third and top

Bob Berry, the would-be record-breaker, was back on the beach in May, 1953, his ambitions still running high. He was talking, not just of breaking the new record that had been set up in December by another German, W Herz, on an NSU at 180.17 mph, but of cracking the 200 and 300 mph barrier! But not on Pendine. 150 mph, he reckoned, was about Pendine's limit, for a motor cycle. He would need to look abroad, to the 12-mile long expanse of the dried salt lake at Bonneville, Utah. Pendine would, in future, be his test-track.

He had burned a great deal of 'midnight oil' to produce a potent, 'all-enveloped' record breaker. Its greatest innovation was the adaptation of the frame to a 'prone', semi-kneeling, riding position.[3] This configuration, now world-famous, was in fact imitated from American Vincent rider, Roland 'Rollie' Free, who adopted it for record runs at Bonneville. Rollie Free calculated on a speed-increase dividend of between 17 and 20 mph above 140 mph. The thinking behind the Brough's fish-tailed, bullet-shaped Electron alloy shell, based on Fernihough's streamlined OEC - which Berry considered sound for 250mph, was based on doing battle with 'wind-resistance'. It was aerodynamically unscientific, as he was to discover.

Hairpin valve springs replaced the coil-springs of the proprietary JAP (JTOR) head. This, according to Berry, made a tremendous difference.[4] Compression ratios were up to 14.5 to 1 on the front, and 14.2 to 1 on the rear cylinder - the front being the cooler-running. The power-output of the JAP-twin was thereby up-rated to 90 bhp at 6 700 rpm. Stan Greening, JA Prestwich's designer, even ran it on the dynamometer at 7 400rpm and the con-rods held! The standard light-alloy racing cylinder heads had been replaced by cast-iron ones to facilitate quicker warming-up. Induction to the twin carburettors was via air intake scoops and ram tubes. It was estimated that the scoops

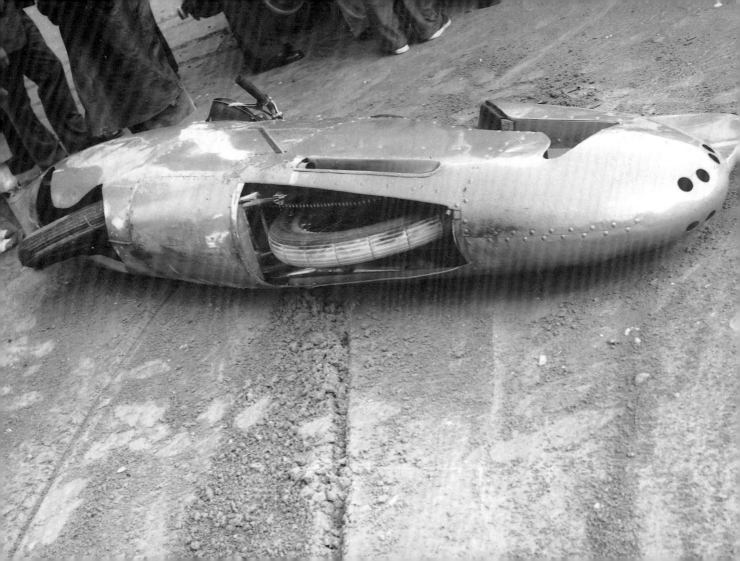

contributed an extra 10 bhp at speeds above 160 mph. The Renolds chains, which took a tremendous bashing, were drip-lubricated.

A special heavy-duty clutch was built to counter slip on take-off and at high speed and, on Dunlop's advice, Berry swapped the duralumin wheels for steel, with rolled-thread spokes. 70psi pressures were recommended with the special mix sand-grip speed-record tyres. Dunlop had provided 8-ply silk cord walled tyres of 3.50 x12 ins, with only ⅛ inches of smooth tread as a precaution against 'tread throw'. Berry was full of praise for Dunlops' unstinting help throughout his career as an aspiring record-breaker.

The idea was to test-run his new machine in July, again without the light-alloy streamlined shell and, given that 160 mph came up without problems (in second gear!), he intended to go back and run it on the road at Jabbecke near Ostende or on the autobahn near Munich to be officially timed with the streamlining in place. By his calculation,

not verified by wind-tunnel trials, the streamlining would give him an extra 40 mph. The 'sand-drag' factor had variously been assessed at reducing speed by between 10 and 15%. Taking these factors into account he would have been looking at a speed of 240 mph on the road. Considering the guess-work and absence of advanced aero-dynamics, Berry was fortunate he never got there!

During a practice session he foolishly took the machine for 'a spin' up the course, wearing only beach clothes. At 167 mph, with the fairing in place, he got into trouble. A half-mile wobble ensued. He lost it - and came off: lucky to come out of it alive. Carmarthen hospital treated his fractured skull and collar-bone, his smashed teeth and broken toes. His spirit was not broken.

[3]George Tucker, in 1929, had modified an AJW Super Four, with a blown 985cc British Anzani engine, into the 'First of the Kneelers' for Brooklands. There is nothing new!

[4]From BB's hand-written ms. notes for what might be a first-draft autobiography, via B Thredder.

4. *All-out*

Bob Berry, licking his wounds, disappeared from view for a good few years. Still doggedly canvassing sponsorship, he was back in 1959. The Land Speed Record for motor cycles had progressed somewhat, but was in a muddle at 211 or 214 mph. NSU and Triumph were in legal contention.

He had done some serious thinking, abandoned the kneeler, the fish-tailed 'bullet' based on the remnants of the fabulous old Jack Carr-derived Brough racer, in favour of a 1920s chassis, the OEC-Temple-Reynolds, made famous by Claude Temple and Joe Wright at Brooklands and elsewhere. This long, and somewhat cumbersome-looking, machine had been involved in the record-attempt scandal on a road near Cork, in Eire. There, in 1930, Wright and his team claimed to have achieved a World Record of 150.74 mph on the Carrigrohane Straight. When the machine was exhibited at Olympia, it was revealed by a witness that the OEC-Temple had only completed half the record run. A gudgeon pin had broken, putting it out of contention for the obligatory return dash, due within an hour. The 'spare' machine, a Zenith, had (cheatingly) been brought in to service!

JAPs supplied Berry with a new engine. Its cylinder heads and barrels were of light alloy, sparked by twin racing magnetos and fed by twin Amal carburettors. Its Duplex front suspension was damped by the addition of Girling shock absorbers. An extended rear sub-frame had been welded on to the OEC-Temple-Reynolds frame to carry outrigger footrests and controls, the engine being mounted behind the driver. The linkage to the 4-speed Burman (racing Norton) gearbox had a similar hand/foot change to the earlier version.

The whole was enveloped in a specially designed and wind-tunnel-tested bright crimson, streamlined fibreglass shell, christened variously 'The Whale', 'Moby Dick' and 'The Projectile' by the press, but

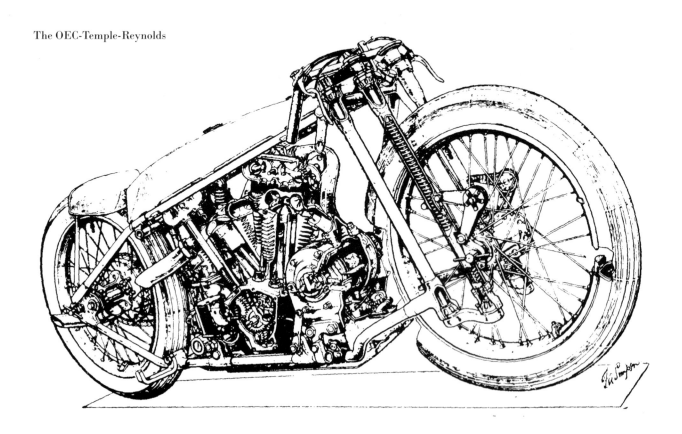

which Berry referred to as 'The Streamliner'. Fifteen feet long, it was designed by Jim Livesey, a mechanical science lecturer at Manchester University, and fabricated from resins supplied by British Resin Products, at HP Pressurecast Ltd, Manchester, a plastics firm which supplied de Havilands. The overall height of the shell was no more than 36 inches, allowing 4 inches ground-clearance. In all appearance it is a fuselage without wings.

An important sponsorship deal that he had been relying on had meanwhile fallen through, and Berry found himself in difficulties. He and Harry Sefton had formed a partnership, 'Bob Berry Enterprises, Ltd, World Record Attempt, 1958', with EC Mudie, of Finvoy Garage, Liverpool. This enterprise foundered.

A fund-raiser poster

p.34 The OEC-Temple on the Carrigrohane Road, Cork, 1930

p.35 Bob Berry working on the OEC-Temple, 1959

Among the commercial sponsorships he had managed to secure for his proposed sortie to Utah were help 'in kind' from JAP engines, Amal carburettors, Mobil oil, Terry Aero valve springs, Lucas ignition, Champion spark plugs, ICI paints, British Resin Products, HP Pressurecast, Ltd, Ferodo linings and Dunlops. But Berry needed 'hard cash' backing to continue development and get him to Utah in August or early September. NSU had put their resources behind Wilhelm Hertz and Triumph had backed the American, Johnny Allen. He could find no one to share his vision. No British capital was ever forthcoming.

Having invested more than 4000 hours in development work, Bob Berry spent five weeks at Pendine in the summer of 1959, when a combination of beach and weather conditions only met his criteria three times. He was assisted by, among others, a faithful volunteer, Bill Kirkby, who rode down daily

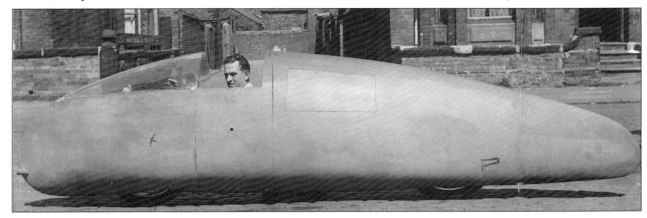

'The Streamliner', aka 'Moby Dick' or 'The Projectile', Manchester, 1959

from Pontrhydfendigaid in mid-Wales. In response to an advertisement, a team of - mainly girl - 'catchers' was in attendance to hold the machine. He had run so short of money that he was obliged to change his hotel room for modest digs in Laugharne. The 'Pendine & District Bob Berry Fund' tried to raise some money for him through local dances and whist-drives. So uninhibited - or desperate - was Berry that, after an appeal on Granada television, he resorted to 'begging-bowl' tactics at Silverstone, the Isle-of-man and Oulton Park - which brought derision on his head from some quarters. It was a 'do-or-die' situation, but still he did not give up.

*

Berry was back again in the autumn of 1960. A patient development engineer, he had been able to identify minor changes to the fairing that would strengthen the screen and assist access and egress. Fuel expert, Charles Vermes came down from London. The motor was now said to be producing a

p.37 'Streamliner', 1959

p.39 Schoolboy admirers

very-near-to-bursting-point 105 bhp at 6 800 rpm, a power-to-weight ratio of 370bhp per ton.[5] This, he maintained (somehow), would receive a boost of up to 45% from the dry-ice-packed ram-ducts to the carburettors when his speed rose above 140mph.

Running on a mixture of pump fuel and ethol/methyl, he says he saw the equivalent of 200 mph on the rev counter in third gear (186mph on the ASI), and eased off - only to have the OEC-Temple-JAP cockpit fill with gas. With red-hot exhausts enclosed within the Streamliner's cowling, he was riding a two-wheeled bomb! He must have had a fright.

*

Berry's personal account of his final test run at Pendine, which appeared in *The Motor Cycle* in edited form, is as follows:

38

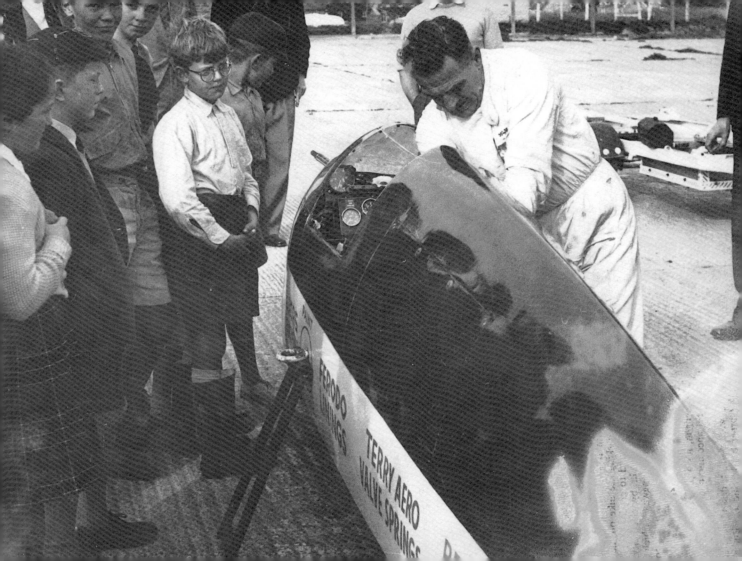

Let me try and explain the Pendine set-up and its faults and virtues. When in perfect condition the beach is quite probably as good as Bonneville Salt Flats but of course much shorter, the longest stretch I have ever been able to use being five miles. Now for the snags.

The beach can roughly be divided into 2 sections, the first stretch three miles long being usually almost, or quite, perfect, but the farthest two miles, beyond where the sandhills end and the coastline curves inland, are suitable for 150 mph plus perhaps, once in a fortnight. The beach can be perfect at dawn and after a midday tide can be hopeless. It can be in perfect condition for two or three tides but unusable because of cross winds which prevail.

The beach runs from east to west. At dawn the rising sun completely blinds a rider travelling towards the east. At sunset it is perhaps worse in the opposite direction. And usually at dawn and dusk it is windless. Sir Malcolm Campbell spent three months waiting for favourable conditions on one of his record attempts. Amy Johnson and Jim Mollison waited six weeks in (Seafarer) before taking off on their epic trip to America from the famous beach.

In 1959 I waited five weeks and the fastest speed I could attain was 154 mph in second gear, due to soft beaches and three rows of steel posts which run diagonally across my track. These posts spaced 100 yards apart are used for artillery ranges by the Government establishment which uses the beach for weapons testing. Due to having to drive through the posts at an acute angle, the maximum clearance between them and the beach is 10 feet. The posts are almost invisible when approached in a car at 70 mph.

In a streamliner at 150 mph and above, it is impossible to see them at all. When one takes into account that the projectile cannot be steered at over 90 mph thus preventing any possibility of steering round them the posts constitute a bit of a hazard. I returned to Pendine this year to see if I could top 180 mph and thus reach a speed higher than has ever been attained before on land in Britain, and at the same time to see if the bike stayed straight at this speed. I needed this assurance before going to Bonneville as I have always been against travelling to America with an untried project and should hate to come unstuck in front of 160 million Americans, quite a lot of whom purchase British motorcycles.

This visit to Pendine differed in several ways from previous trials there. First, I had never been so late in the year as most of my previous trials and official attempts at the old record had taken place in July and August at dawn and dusk, that is around 6 am and 8 pm. This time I planned to run in the late mornings, wind and beach permitting.

Until 1959 I had, when not on officially timed runs, been forced to rely on rev counter reading for speeds reached, but of course could not rely on the absolute accuracy of these due to a certain amount of wheel spin on the sand. We realised that at higher speeds than 150 mph, due to the increased wind resistance, wheel slip would be even greater and I wanted accurate speeds for data purposes and drag calculations, it was realised that some other method of speed recording would have to be used. Officially measured distances and timing could not be used due to the fact that any speeds in the region of 180 - 190 mph would be of the duration of only five seconds during which time I would have travelled over a quarter of a mile. Due to the extremely good streamlining of the machine, when the throttle is closed, the speed hardly drops, it just keeps going on at a hell of a bat. There is no front brake and if the rear brake is used at over 100mph it would only lock the wheel and perhaps start a slide. The problem would not arise at Bonneville due to the length of the record strips (12 miles), but at Pendine the slightest delay in shutting off could easily

Cockpit of the OEC-Temlpe. Engine rear

Trial-run. Spring, 1959

end up with the bike smashing into the cliffs at one end of the beach or running into the estuary at the other end. Quite sticky! Hence the vital need for a dead accurate instrument registering the speed irrespective of wheel spin and also of whichever gear the machine was using, second or third, (it is impossible to get into top gear at Pendine). The answer was an air speed indicator and pilot head from an aeroplane. One was supplied by an enthusiast from Nottingham and was tested and calibrated at Manchester University. The pilot head was fitted to the nose

43

Pendine, 1960. Just before the '186mph pass'

of the machine, projecting 2-6" in front of it where it would be in still air and the 4" dial placed in the nose of the perspex canopy where it could be easily seen whilst travelling at any speed. The pilot head looks like a 20mm cannon on a Spitfire wing and caused many a head to be scratched!

But in operation it is the complete answer to my problems. It is extremely sensitive to the slightest change in speed. When the bike is being towed on the trailer behind my car the air speed needle is registering the speed on the road of the car and trailer.

After waiting fifteen weeks for good weather reports from South Wales, I decided in October to take a chance and go down to Pendine and wait for a favourable opportunity to get in at least two fast runs.

Most amazingly I left Manchester in blazing sunshine on the first day of what proved to be an 'Indian summer' and upon arrival at Pendine found we could not use the beach until the Saturday following due to the Ministry of supply holding night exercises on it.

We were on he beach at 8 am on the Saturday morning in bright sunshine but with a strong breeze blowing offshore at right angles to my course.

We drove along the beach in the car on a 'survey trip' to lay off a suitable course. The sands were in better condition than I had ever seen them and a course was selected on the tide line left by the last tide. The entire length of sand usable was 4.6 miles and necessitated having to travel through three lines of the hated steel posts. We returned to the Pendine end of the beach and unloaded the quarter ton bike from the trailer. Everything was prepared for an instant start and the party sat down to watch the windsock on the beach which was hanging at an angle of 45 degrees. Until that windsock was almost vertical, I dared not ride the bike. Side area of the machine is 150 square feet, she would curve off course and finish up in the sea.

As the sun became hotter, the wind dropped noticeably and at 11.15 we decided that at 11.30 I would get cracking if the wind dropped a little more. At 11.30 I climbed into the cockpit and put on my crash helmet and glare goggles and in that minute, most dramatically the windsock dropped against its pole. Petrol taps were turned on, the bike was pulled back onto compression and then pushed forward. I dropped the clutch and the engine fired at once. I drove the bike across the beach for 200 yards down to the tideline and curved onto the course, gradually opening up and sighting the distant mountains as a course marker. Slowly opening up, the air speed needle swung round to 100 in bottom gear, a quick change into second and still accelerating slowly up to 150mph as I strained to see those steel posts. There they were, and thank heaven I was not heading for them. I flashed through them and opened up until 165 mph showed on the air speed indicator. The exhaust noise was terrific, even inside the cockpit. A quick glance at the instrument panel and as I looked ahead I could see a tiny black dot in the distance. The Land Rover which we were using as a course end marker. I closed the throttle but the Rover rapidly grew in size. Down to 70mph and on with the brake. Down to 10mph. The 'catch crew' ran forward but on an impulse I steered the bike down towards the sea and then turned in an 80 foot circle and turned back towards Pendine 4½ miles away and quite invisible in the distance. I lined the bike up on the 500-foot cliff at the end of the beach and opened the throttle. On this run I was determined, posts or no posts, to really have a go as there would be no time for further runs as the tide was coming in fast and would cover the track I was using. I particularly wanted to exceed 175 mph, as this was the fastest speed ever recorded on land in the British Isles and would tell me all I wanted to know about the stability of the bike.

Up to 80 mph the bike was rolling a little but as she went 'off the handlebars' and on to the streamlining at 100 mph she became rock steady. Change into second gear at 115 and still accelerating at lightning speed. Fully committed now on its course and unable to change direction, we hurtled towards Pendine, 165 on the air speed indicator and into third. 170 -175 and the bike rock steady, 180 and the wind was shrieking round the cockpit, the exhaust not so loud now, a beautifully smooth noise from the engine room at my back. A large tree branch right in my track, I know I cannot avoid it, instinctively I brace myself, a distinct thump and we are over it. The ASI reaches 186 mph and the rev counter shows 200 mph. I wonder why the difference? Wheelspin, of course. I count up to five slowly, that's a quarter of a mile. The distant cliff is flying at me and I cut the throttle back and at once I think I have left

it too late. The beach is shrinking unbelievably quickly, 150 - 140 130. The cliff is huge now. I can see the village. Down to 80 and into bottom gear and gently on with the brake, the cockpit is filled with a choking smell of alcohol, ether and nitro benzine. It makes me cough and gasp for air.

The nitro affects my vision and the ether makes me dizzy. Slowly the streamliner loses its speed and with only 300 yards to spare, I stop alongside my two 'catchers' and switch off the big engine. The cockpit reeks of dope and hot oil. I climb out and glance at my watch: 11.35. Just five minutes since I left. A round trip of nine miles. I look at the incoming tide, it is too close to chance another run. But I am more than satisfied. As we stand round the bike, I look towards the windsock. It suddenly billows out and rises to 45 degrees and the wind blows sand devils along the beach. For five minutes there had been just a perfect flat calm!

Strange to think that after five years of building this beautiful monster, her total 'working' life may, in all, be perhaps half an hour!

All to no avail. Bob Berry and his Land Speed project had somehow begun to lose credibility.

[5]Formula One GP racing cars of the time had a p/w ratio of between 400 and 425bhp per ton.

5. Reverse

Idolised by some, reviled by others, Bob Berry's name is indelibly entered in Pendine's ledger more for his effort on the beach than his achievement. He was a patient development engineer, and there is no denying his inventiveness and competence as an engine-tuner. The standard of his preparation work and the finish with which he imbued his machines were top-class - considering his very limited resources[6].

With benefit of hindsight, there is little doubt that Berry's concepts were flawed and doomed to failure in the long run. The first record-breaker's shell, the old Brough Superior, was unscientific and had inherent high-speed stability problems. It may have been 'streamlined', but it was not 'aerodynamic'.

His loyalty to an engine designed before the Great War seems misplaced, especially in 1960, considering the very high stresses to which he was proposing to subject the 998cc JAP V-twin, while expecting reliability. The OEC-Temple Streamliner was, nevertheless, basically a remarkably powerful machine - and fast. If that had been the only consideration - perhaps sufficiently so to have broken the record.

But in a situation where the bike went 'off the handlebars' at 90+mph, Berry was axiomatically proceeding out of control at anything beyond that speed. He had no front brake - and at very high speed, with wheels off the ground part of the time, there was real danger in using the rear brake.

The lessons in aerodynamics to be learned from fighter aircraft design were required if he was to be serious about speeds in excess of 200mph, much less 300mph.[7] With no high-speed steering - a rudder - and no means of applying downward pressures, via ailerons, when the projectile tended towards 'lift-off', he was staring at catastrophe.

On Pendine beach, steel marker-posts lay in his path, and the least breeze could have sent him careering into the dunes - or a watery grave.

Ideally, computer-controlled 'Active' suspension, common enough today, would have assisted stability and wheel-spin problems. This was unknown in 1960, but in any future wheel-propelled World Land Speed Record attempt it will need to be a first consideration.

As a racing motorcyclist, Bob Berry's record on Pendine is somewhat disappointing. He had begun racing 'up North' in 1931 on an Ivory Calthorpe, later a 490 Norton, but did not race on Pendine until after the war. He then became a regular, between 1946 and his 'retirement' from racing in 1948. He always appeared impeccably turned out, in white overalls, with the highly-polished Brough Superior and an equally venerable 'Inter' Norton. The successes he scored were somewhat lowly. In the 'pecking order' of Pendine racers he emerges overall no higher than 27th, among the 'amateurs'. He made one 'reprise' appearance in August, 1952, on a Triumph Thunderbird, intended to intimidate Fred Rist; but to no avail. It happened to be a day when Rex Young, with a works 541cc Featherbed Manx Norton, had wings on his heels!

Despite concentrated fund-raising and still more development, Bob Berry never got his 'Streamliner' to the Salt Lake, Utah. He knew that his Manchester-based rival, Reg Dearden, was preparing a supercharged Vincent for an assault on the flying kilo and mile. Dearden tested his machine on Pendine, breaking a crank-pin in the process - and encountering the high-speed instability problem.

There were rumours of other contenders, some with factory-backing.

p.51& 53 Manchester garage of 'World's Fastest Motorcyclist'

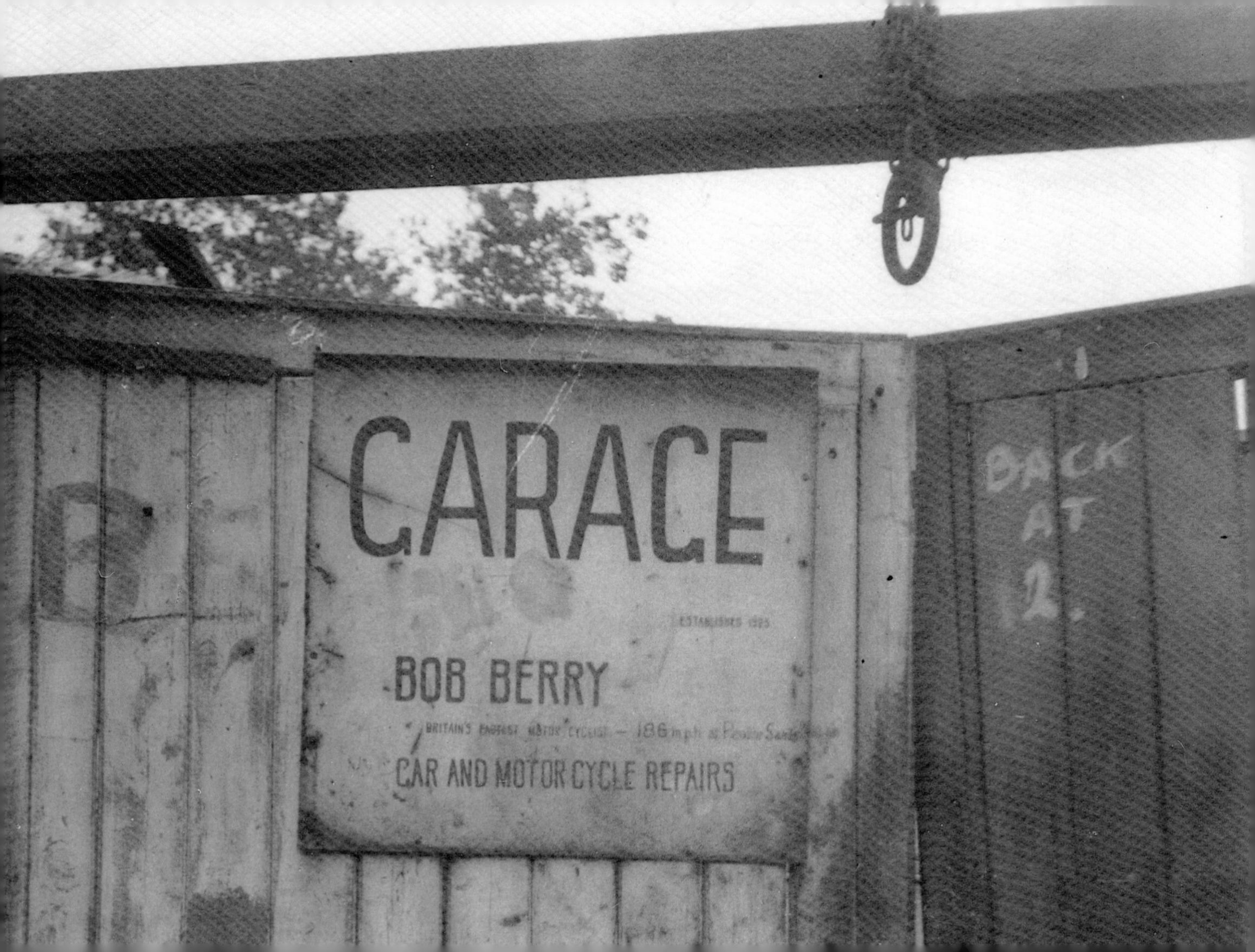
GARAGE
BOB BERRY
CAR AND MOTOR CYCLE REPAIRS
BACK AT 12.

All Bob Berry's efforts and resources he had invested in his obsessional and single-handed ambition to be the fastest man on two wheels, for Britain. He failed for lack of resources, being behind in technology and simple lack of cash.

In poor health and burdened by debt, Berry retired from his back-street garage in Manchester, with the painted wooden sign: 'The World's Fastest Motorcyclist'. He came to live in obscurity with his friend, Peggy Carodus, on a remote small-holding in Tegryn, Carmarthenshire. Like many another from the other side of Offa's Dyke, Bob was in a love affair with Pendine, albeit unrequited, that never would let go. He died of 'an embolism of the stomach', in 1970, at Glangwili Hospital, Carmarthen, at the age of 62.

Malcolm Campbell had registered 184mph on the Railton Blue Bird's instruments on Pendine, in 1927. Bob Berry says he saw 186mph on the OEC-Temple-JAP's Air Speed Indicator, in 1960: thus claiming the fastest 'unofficial' speed attained on the beach - in one direction - and on mainland Britain at that time.

⁶When visited by De Haviland executives, they were astonished by the revelation that a hole in Berry's work-bench was his method of pipe-bending!
⁷These had not yet been incorporated into production car or racing car design; though sports-racing cars, achieving speeds of up to 200mph, had begun to take cognisance of the necessity. Bristols, in particular, leading the way with their Le Mans entries.

GARAGE

BOB DERRY

Acknowledgements

For help along the way with the piecing together of the story of Bob Berry's association with Pendine, the author would like to acknowledge the help, guidance and courtesy of: Henry Adams, Titch Allen (VMCC), Mike Budd (National Motor Museum, Beaulieu), Roland Carr, Raymond Davies (Ashwell Garage, Pendine), Bruce Eynon, Ken George, Dave James, Mike Leatherdale (Brough Superior Club), Hugh Moffat, Denis Parkinson, Ivan Rhodes (Rhodes Collection), DD Snow, Bob Thredder, Brian Willis and Mike Worthington-Williams.

Photographs are principally by courtesy of Bob Thredder from the Bob Berry collection, relict of Mrs Peggy Carodus. For some others thanks are due to: Carmarthen Museum; Peter John, for his father, Ken John's, fine action study of JH Carr (Brough Superior); and to Roland Carr for the picture of his father on Pendine in 1932, from the JH Carr collection. Wayne Bowen kindly contributed the classic shot of Bob Berry on the 'JH Carr Brough' on Pendine in 1946, by LA Lusardi of Nantymoel. Thanks also to John Lusardi.